Documenting Change

Documenting Change

Essential Strategies for Managing Cost Escalations in Construction

Robert West

To my dad, Bob West, whose boundless patience and unwavering love shaped who I am. His guidance, wisdom, and dedication to instilling the highest work ethic in me made this book possible. I am forever grateful for his passion and the invaluable lessons he's imparted.

To my family, whose unwavering support and understanding made this journey possible.

To my wife, Sheila, for her endless patience and encouragement, and for allowing me the time and space to bring this book to life. Without your love and belief in me, this accomplishment would not have been possible.

Table Of Contents

CHAPTER 1

Understanding Cost Escalation in Construction

What Exactly is Cost Escalation?

Let's start with the basics: cost escalation in construction is when the expenses for a project exceed the original budget. This can happen for a number of reasons—anything from market fluctuations and rising material costs to labor shortages or unexpected issues at the site. If you're a construction project manager, subcontractor, or vendor, knowing how to anticipate and handle these cost escalations is key to staying on track and keeping the project profitable. By recognizing early warning signs and planning accordingly, you'll be better prepared to manage resources efficiently and deliver successful outcomes.

One major factor behind cost escalation is the unpredictability of material prices. Whether it's steel, lumber, or concrete, these essential commodities can experience price swings due to global supply chain issues, economic shifts, or increased local demand. The most innovative project managers keep a close eye on market trends and adapt their contracts to allow for price adjustments. Building relationships with suppliers or securing long-term deals can also soften the blow when prices spike unexpectedly.

Labor Costs: A Big Piece of the Puzzle

Labor is another huge driver of cost escalation. The construction industry can regularly face a shortage of skilled workers, which pushes wages up. And when wages rise, so do your project costs. On top of that, new regulations—like labor laws or updated safety requirements—can mean extra expenses for training or workforce management. Staying ahead of these challenges is crucial, specifically to track trends in the labor market and invest in workforce development programs that boost efficiency and productivity.

Surprises on the Site: More Than Just a Minor Setback

It's not uncommon for a project to hit bumps in the road when unexpected site conditions arise—think surprise soil issues, hidden utility lines, or even weather that doesn't cooperate. These unforeseen obstacles can throw a wrench in the schedule and drive up costs. The best way to tackle this? Thorough site assessments and risk management strategies before breaking ground. Keeping detailed records of any changes and their impact on the budget will help you justify cost adjustments and keep stakeholders in the loop.

Why Material Costs Fluctuate

One of the biggest reasons costs go up in construction is due to the unpredictable nature of material prices. If your project relies on key materials like steel, lumber, or concrete, you've probably noticed how dramatically their prices can change. Factors like global supply chain disruptions, economic conditions, and even local demand can cause huge price swings. For project managers and subcontractors, it's important to stay informed about these trends. One way to reduce risk is by working flexible pricing strategies into your contracts or setting up long-term agreements with suppliers. That way, if prices start to climb, you won't be blindsided.

Labor Costs: Another Moving Target

Labor costs are another big contributor to cost escalation. The construction industry often struggles with labor shortages, which means companies have to pay more to attract skilled workers. On top of that, regulations like new labor laws or safety requirements can mean additional costs for workforce training and management. Smart project managers keep an eye on labor market trends and anticipate potential shortages. By being proactive—such as investing in workforce training programs that increase productivity—you can help control costs even when wages rise.

The Surprises That Can Throw You Off Track

It is a rare occurrence to have a construction project go exactly as you have planned, and site conditions are a big reason why. Whether it's discovering unexpected soil issues, hitting hidden utilities, or being delayed by bad weather, unforeseen problems can disrupt schedules and increase costs. That's where thorough planning and risk management come in. By conducting site assessments early and putting contingency plans in place, you can anticipate these issues before they turn into costly delays. And when you do encounter surprises, keeping a clear and detailed record of what went wrong will make it easier to explain cost increases to your clients or partners.

The Importance of Documentation

Finally, having good documentation is a game-changer when it comes to managing cost escalations. Keeping track of every contract, change order, and conversation is key to justifying any necessary budget increases. With an organized documentation system, you'll be able to present a solid case for additional funding, ensuring that everyone involved understands why costs have gone up.

When you know how to document changes and explain cost escalations clearly, you can navigate even the most complex projects with greater confidence and success.

When you know how to document changes and explain cost escalations clearly, you can navigate even the most complex projects with greater confidence and success.

Common Causes of Cost Increases

Cost overruns are not always avoidable, but knowing the most common causes can help you prepare and respond better. Here's a quick rundown of why construction projects often face cost increases:

1. **Material Price Fluctuations:** As mentioned earlier, the prices for materials like steel or lumber can change drastically due to global events, supply chain issues, or sudden changes in demand. For example, natural disasters or geopolitical tensions can lead to shortages, pushing prices up unexpectedly.
2. **Labor Shortages:** The construction industry often faces a shortage of skilled workers, which drives up wages. This, combined with regulatory changes like new labor laws, can add to your project's expenses.
3. **Project Scope Changes:** Sometimes clients request changes or additions to the original project plan after work has already started. These changes, known as scope creep, can lead to increased material costs, labor hours, and even delays.
4. **Regulatory Changes:** New regulations, whether environmental, safety-related, or building code updates, can add unexpected costs to a project. It's important to stay ahead of these changes and factor them into your planning.
5. **Economic Factors:** Inflation and interest rates can also affect your costs. As inflation rises, the value of your budget decreases, making materials and labor more expensive.
6. **Interest rate changes:** can affect your financing costs, making it more costly to borrow money for construction projects.

The Impact of Cost Escalation on Projects

When project costs start climbing, the effects are felt across the board. Cost escalation can put a serious strain on your project's budget, timeline, and even relationships with stakeholders. Let's take a closer look at how these cost increases can impact a construction project:

Budget Strain

One of the most immediate challenges is how escalating costs stretch the budget .As expenses grow, project managers are often forced to scramble for additional funding, whether that means renegotiating with clients, seeking financing, or reallocating resources from other projects.

It's a stressful situation that can lead to rushed decisions and, in some cases, mistakes. But having a solid documentation trail can make things easier. By keeping clear records of what's driving the cost increases, you'll have a stronger case when asking for more money.

Project Delays

Cost escalation doesn't just affect the bottom line—it can also throw your schedule off track. Delays in securing additional funding or adjusting the project scope can lead to extended timelines. For contractors working with the federal government or on tightly scheduled projects, these delays can have serious consequences. Penalties, higher labor costs, and even strained relationships with clients are all potential outcomes. This is why proactive communication and solid documentation are so important—they help you maintain transparency and trust throughout the project, even when things get tough.

Reputation Risks

Projects that see significant cost increases can also suffer from reputational damage. Stakeholders, including clients and regulatory bodies, may start questioning your competence if the project goes way over budget or schedule. For smaller contractors or those working under government set-asides, maintaining a good reputation is critical to securing future work. The best way to protect your reputation is by implementing and sticking to best practices for documenting cost escalations. When you can clearly show why costs increased and how you managed the situation, you demonstrate professionalism and accountability.

CHAPTER 2

Importance
of
Documentation

The Role of Documentation in Cost Management

Documentation serves as the backbone for managing costs in construction projects. It ensures that every decision, every change, and every transaction is recorded, providing a clear audit trail that can be referred to throughout the project lifecycle. Effective documentation not only helps track expenses but also facilitates communication, justifies cost increases, and prevents disputes among stakeholders.

In an industry where costs can escalate due to unforeseen circumstances, maintaining a detailed record of expenditures and decisions is essential for maintaining control over the project budget. Comprehensive documentation allows project managers, subcontractors, and vendors to proactively identify trends and mitigate risks. With a well-documented history, it becomes easier to manage cost fluctuations and explain them to stakeholders, ensuring that everyone is aligned on all project goals.

Documentation as a Tool for Financial Tracking and Communication

Accurate record-keeping allows construction managers to track cost increases as they happen, and understand their underlying causes. These records enable managers to make data-driven decisions, whether it's adjusting the scope of work, shifting resources, or communicating cost increases to clients. Timely and organized documentation also supports communication with all stakeholders—clients, subcontractors, and regulatory bodies—fostering transparency and trust.

In many cases, particularly in federal government contracts or small business set-aside programs, documentation is more than a best practice; it's a contractual requirement. Failure to comply with documentation guidelines—such as the submission of change orders or evidence of incurred expenses—can result in delayed payments, disputes, or even the loss of contracts. A thorough documentation system is not just a safeguard against budget overruns; it's critical to project success.

Legal Implications of Inadequate Documentation

In construction, inadequate documentation can lead to significant legal consequences. When project managers fail to keep comprehensive records, they expose themselves to disputes and legal claims. Whether it's a disagreement over contract terms, delays, or budget increases, clear documentation can make or break a legal case.

Breach of Contract and Disputes Over Scope Changes

One of the primary legal risks of poor documentation is the difficulty in substantiating claims for additional costs. In many projects, contractors may be entitled to compensation for unforeseen circumstances that lead to cost escalations. However, without proper documentation—such as approved change orders, daily logs, and correspondence—it becomes nearly impossible to prove the legitimacy of those claims. As a result, denied claims can lead to costly litigation, tarnishing relationships with clients and jeopardizing future business opportunities.

Additionally, the absence of thorough documentation can undermine compliance with federal regulations and contractual obligations. For government vendors, adherence to documentation requirements is critical for payment eligibility and avoiding penalties. A lack of compliance documentation, whether it relates to safety standards, project schedules, or material specifications, can result in disqualification from future contracts or, worse, legal action from regulatory bodies.

Courts Rely on Documentation

When a legal dispute occurs, courts will often follow the principle of "whoever fails to document, fails to protect." Clear, transparent records of all project activities, decisions, and communications are critical when attempting to resolve disputes. Without these records, construction professionals risk facing adverse judgments. To protect themselves, project managers must adopt comprehensive documentation practices from the start of every project.

Benefits of Thorough Documentation

Beyond dispute resolution, thorough documentation is a strategic asset that drives project success. It offers clear benefits in terms of accountability, communication, and financial management. Let's explore the most critical advantages of meticulous record-keeping in construction projects.

1. **Mitigating Disputes and Avoiding Miscommunications:** Disputes are a common occurrence in construction, whether due to misunderstandings, changes in scope, or disagreements over costs. Having detailed records that document every decision and change throughout the project lifecycle helps clarify what was agreed upon and by whom. This transparency prevents miscommunications, facilitates faster dispute resolution, and reduces the possibility of costly legal battles.

2. **Transparency With Stakeholders:** Clear documentation fosters transparency across the entire project team. When clients, subcontractors, and government vendors all have access to the same information, there's less room for misinterpretation. This openness promotes collaboration and keeps everyone aligned on project timelines, scope, and financial expectations. Transparent documentation practices are essential for maintaining trust and creating smoother project execution.

3. **Supporting Financial Management and Forecasting:** Financial documentation goes beyond tracking current expenses; it helps project managers forecast future costs. By meticulously recording expenses related to labor, materials, and equipment, project managers can analyze trends that inform future budgeting decisions. Historical data becomes a powerful tool when negotiating contracts, securing financing, or planning future projects.

4. **Ensuring Compliance with Industry Standards and Regulations:** Many construction projects, especially those involving federal contracts or public funding, are subject to stringent documentation requirements. Thorough documentation ensures compliance with these regulations, protecting your firm from potential penalties and positioning your company as a reliable partner. Meeting documentation mandates not only helps avoid fines but also enhances your company's reputation and competitiveness in the marketplace.

Embracing Technology to Enhance Documentation Practices

The complexity of modern construction projects makes manual documentation increasingly difficult to manage. Fortunately, technology offers tools that simplify the documentation process, ensuring that records are complete, accurate, and accessible. By embracing modern project management software, construction professionals can streamline the documentation process, improve efficiency, and ultimately drive project success.

Automating Documentation for Accuracy and Accessibility

Digital documentation tools offer features such as real-time expense tracking, automated alerts when budgets are exceeded, and centralized document storage. These tools reduce the likelihood of human error, minimize the time spent on record-keeping, and ensure that all project stakeholders can access up-to-date information whenever necessary.

Real-Time Data and Analytics

Many project management platforms now offer real-time data and analytics, allowing project managers to spot cost increases as soon as they occur. This data-driven approach enables proactive decision-making, whether it involves addressing productivity issues, renegotiating with suppliers, or adjusting project timelines to avoid further delays.

Conclusion: Documentation as a Strategic Advantage

Effective documentation is much more than an administrative task; it's a powerful tool that drives success in construction. By maintaining accurate and comprehensive records, project managers can justify cost increases, avoid disputes, and ensure compliance with contractual obligations. Clear documentation supports better communication, enhances financial management, and positions firms for long-term success.

In an industry where costs can escalate unexpectedly, thorough documentation is your best defense. It protects your company from legal risks, fosters trust with stakeholders, and lays the foundation for successful project completion. By prioritizing systematic and transparent documentation practices, construction professionals can navigate the complexities of modern projects with confidence and achieve greater financial stability.

CHAPTER 3

Best Practices for Documenting Cost Increases

Establishing a Documentation Protocol

Creating a clear and structured protocol for documentation is essential if you want to manage cost increases effectively. When everyone on your team follows the same system for recording and storing project information, it improves accountability and transparency. This consistent approach helps avoid confusion, speeds up decision-making, and makes it easier to resolve conflicts down the line.

The first step in setting up a good documentation protocol is identifying the types of documents that need to be created and maintained. These might include contracts, change orders, payment applications, correspondence, and daily logs. Each document should have a specific purpose and follow a consistent format so that all the necessary details are captured. For example, daily logs should include things like weather conditions, progress updates, and any incidents on-site that could impact the project. Having this information recorded can help support claims for cost increases later on.

Keeping Documentation Updated and Accurate

Once you've determined what needs to be documented, it's important to establish guidelines for how often documents should be updated and who is responsible for keeping them current. Digital tools can help a lot here, allowing team members to make updates in real-time and ensuring that everyone member of the project has access to the latest project information. Regular training can also reinforce the importance of timely and accurate documentation, encouraging a culture of diligence throughout the project.

Review and Approval Processes

To ensure that your documentation is consistent and accurate, it's essential to have a process in place for reviewing and approving documents. This step helps catch any errors or discrepancies before information is shared with stakeholders. A structured review and approval process also creates a reliable audit trail, which can be invaluable if disputes or questions about cost increases arise later in the project.

Continuous Improvement

Documentation protocols shouldn't be set in stone. They should evolve based on feedback and lessons learned from past projects. Regularly assessing and refining your documentation practices helps you adapt to the unique challenges of each project and improve overall efficiency. Involving your team in this process fosters a collaborative environment and encourages a shared commitment to effective documentation.

Types of Documentation You Need to Manage Cost Escalations

There are several types of documentation that are crucial for managing cost increases effectively. These documents not only protect the interests of everyone involved but also ensure transparency throughout the project lifecycle. Let's take a look at some of the key types on the following page:

1. **Contracts**: The contract is the foundation of any construction project. It outlines the agreed-upon terms, including the project's scope, timeline, and costs. It's critical that everyone involved understands what's expected. A well-drafted contract will also spell out how changes should be documented and approved, which helps avoid confusion and disputes later on.

2. **Change Orders**: When unexpected circumstances arise—like design modifications or unforeseen site conditions—change orders provide a formal way to document and approve these changes. Make sure all change orders are thorough, detailing the reason for the change, the extra costs, and any impact on the project timeline.

3. **Daily Logs**: These might seem like an administrative hassle, but daily logs are one of the best tools for tracking day-to-day activities on-site. They should capture everything from labor hours and materials used to any incidents or delays. By keeping accurate daily logs, you'll have a detailed record that can support claims for cost increases and provide context for why adjustments were needed.

4. **Invoices and Payment Records**: These documents are essential for tracking financial transactions between contractors, subcontractors, and suppliers. Organized and accurate invoices ensure that everyone is held accountable for their financial obligations and help you stay on top of project expenses. Timely payment records can also prevent cash flow issues, which are often a leading cause of cost overruns.

Frequency and Timing of Documentation

When it comes to documenting construction projects, the timing and frequency of your records are just as important as what you document. Staying consistent and timely ensures that any changes, delays, or unforeseen events are captured accurately. This level of attention not only helps keep a clear picture of the project's progress but also strengthens your ability to justify additional costs when needed.

Daily Documentation

One of the most effective ways to keep up with documentation is through daily logs. These records should cover the key events of each day, including workforce attendance, equipment usage, weather conditions, and any notable delays or incidents on-site. By documenting these details daily, you can build a comprehensive account of what's happening on the ground. This kind of real-time logging is especially useful if you need to justify cost increases related to productivity losses or extra labor costs.

Weekly and Monthly Summaries

In addition to daily logs, it's a good idea to create weekly and monthly summaries. These reports should compile the most significant developments from your daily records and offer a broader overview of the project's financial health. Weekly summaries can highlight major issues or progress, while monthly reports can focus on budget variances and forecasts for upcoming costs. These checkpoints allow project managers to step back and assess whether the project is still on track or if adjustments are needed.

Documenting Changes as They Happen

Any alterations to the project's scope, schedule, or budget should be documented immediately. This includes submitting change orders, handling requests for information (RFIs), and communicating with stakeholders about potential cost impacts. Prompt documentation helps create a clear timeline of events and is essential when defending against claims or disputes. By addressing changes as soon as they occur, you maintain transparency and can prevent misunderstandings later in the project.

Using Technology to Streamline Documentation

Technology can often play an important part in improving the frequency and timing of your documentation. Project management software, mobile apps, and cloud-based storage solutions allow teams to update records in real time, making it easier to stay organized. These tools also enable quick sharing of information, and help ensure that everyone involved in the project has access to the most up-to-date data. Embracing these digital solutions makes the documentation process faster, more accurate, and less burdensome for everyone involved.

Why Accurate Documentation is Key to Managing Cost Escalations

Accurate documentation isn't just about keeping records for the sake of it—it's about creating a clear and reliable trail that can help justify cost increases and keep your project on track. Without detailed, up-to-date documentation, managing cost escalations can quickly become overwhelming. Let's look at why getting this right is so important:

1. **Justifying Additional Costs**: If costs rise, you'll need to explain why to clients, stakeholders, or financial backers. Proper documentation shows exactly what went wrong (or changed) and why additional funds are necessary. It helps build a case that is based on facts, not assumptions, which makes it easier to get the approval for increased budgets.

2. **Defending Against Claims**: Disputes over costs are common in construction projects, and they can quickly spiral into larger legal or financial battles if not handled properly. When you have a detailed record of everything that happened on the project—such as change orders, daily logs, and correspondence—you'll be in a stronger position to defend against any claims. This level of transparency can help resolve conflicts before they escalate into costly litigation.

3. **Maintaining Accountability**: By keeping a thorough documentation process in place, you help ensure that everyone involved in the project is accountable. This means contractors, subcontractors, and suppliers are all held to their agreed terms, and any deviations are properly recorded and addressed.

4. **Supporting Future Projects**: The documentation you create for one project can also inform your approach to future work. Analyzing past projects can help you identify common sources of cost escalation and develop strategies to prevent them. Plus, when negotiating new contracts or seeking financing, having detailed records of past projects demonstrates professionalism and reliability.

Establishing a Culture of Consistent Documentation

Getting everyone on your team to take documentation seriously can be a challenge, but it's critical to the success of any project. Here are some best practices for creating a culture of consistent, high-quality documentation:

1. **Set Expectations Early**: Make sure that everyone on your team knows from the outset that documentation is a priority. Clearly communicate what's expected in terms of daily logs, change orders, and other record-keeping practices. Setting these expectations early helps avoid any confusion or resistance later on.

2. **Provide Training**: Not everyone is naturally detail-oriented, especially when it comes to paperwork. Provide training to your team on how to document effectively, what information is most important, and how to use the software or tools you've chosen for the project. The more comfortable they are with the process, the more likely they are to follow through.

3. **Regular Check-Ins**: Make documentation a regular part of your project management meetings. Review what's been recorded, address any gaps or inconsistencies, and ensure that the documentation is aligned with the project's current status.

4. **Recognize the Value of Documentation**: Sometimes people only see documentation as an administrative burden, but helping your team understand how important these records are to the success of the project can shift perspectives. Show them how thorough documentation has helped resolve past issues or justified cost increases to clients—it reinforces the value of their effort.

CHAPTER 4

Tools and Technologies for Documentation

Digital Solutions for Document Management

Planning Ahead to Avoid Surprises

One of the best ways to manage cost escalations is to plan for them before they even happen. While it's impossible to predict every obstacle or expense that might pop up during a construction project, there are several proactive strategies that can help you minimize the impact of cost increases. By anticipating potential challenges and putting safeguards in place, you can keep your project on track and avoid budget overruns.

Conduct Thorough Pre-Construction Assessments

Before you even break ground, a thorough pre-construction assessment is critical. This includes evaluating site conditions, securing necessary permits, and confirming that the design plans are both realistic and detailed. Unforeseen site issues—like poor soil quality or hidden utilities—are some of the biggest culprits behind unexpected cost increases. By performing a comprehensive project site assessment early on, you and your team will have a greater chance of identifying any potential problem areas and be able to adjust your budget accordingly to minimize negative impacts.

Use Your Contingency Budgets Wisely

A well-planned contingency budget is another key to staying ahead of cost escalations. Designating a percentage of the budget specifically for unexpected project expenses ensures that you're prepared for the inevitable surprises that will arise during most construction projects. A common mistake is either not setting a contingency budget or setting one that's too low. The right amount will depend on the complexity and scale of the project, but as a general rule, anywhere between 5% and 15% of the project's total cost is a good place to start.

Keep Communication Channels Open

Cost escalations are often exacerbated by poor communication. If there's a breakdown in communication between stakeholders, small issues can snowball into larger, more expensive problems. Keep communication channels open and ensure that all parties—clients, subcontractors, suppliers—are informed about any changes or issues as soon as they arise. Weekly meetings or progress reports can help maintain transparency ensuring to keep everyone on the same page.

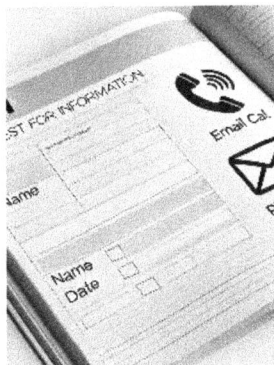

Leverage Technology to Improve Forecasting

One of the most effective ways you can implement to stay ahead of cost increases is by using technology to improve your forecasting. Project management software is very useful when managing construction projects and can help you track expenses in real time and identify trends that could lead to cost increases down the road. These tools also allow you to make more accurate projections about labor needs, material costs, and potential delays, so you can adjust your budget and timeline proactively rather than reactively.

Negotiating Contracts with Flexibility in Mind

Cost escalation is often out of your control, but how you structure your contracts can give you some breathing room when unexpected expenses arise. Negotiating contracts that include flexible terms for material costs, labor, and project timelines can make a huge difference when prices start to climb.

Include Price Adjustment Clauses

A price adjustment clause or escalation clause is a powerful contract tool that allows you to adjust prices if material costs change significantly during the course of the project. This clause helps protect both you and your clients from extreme fluctuations in costs. For instance, if the price of steel suddenly spikes due to a supply chain disruption, the clause allows you to pass on the increase to the client, reducing the financial burden on your company. It's important to discuss these clauses with clients early on, so there are no surprises if they need to be invoked.

Lock in Material Prices Early

Whenever possible, securing fixed prices for key materials can help shield your project from sudden price increases. Fostering strong partnerships with materialmen, vendors, suppliers, and negotiating long-term agreements can often lead to better pricing, especially if you can guarantee repeat business. By securing contracts and purchase orders to lock in prices early, you reduce the risk of budget blowouts down the road.

Incorporate Flexible Timelines

Construction projects rarely stick to their original timelines, especially when cost escalations start to creep in. Having some flexibility in your schedule can ease the pressure when delays arise. By building buffer time into your contracts, you allow room for unforeseen setbacks without the risk of being penalized for missing deadlines.

Managing Stakeholder Expectations

One of the trickiest parts of managing cost escalations is keeping stakeholders in the loop without causing panic. Clients, investors, and partners often have high expectations for the project, and any sign of cost increases can lead to tough conversations. However, being transparent and setting realistic expectations from the start can make these conversations much easier.

Set Clear Expectations from Day One

At the beginning of any project, it's essential to have a frank discussion with your stakeholders about the potential for cost escalations. While no one likes to think about budgets increasing, setting realistic expectations early on can help soften the blow if and when those increases happen. Explain the most common causes of cost escalations, such as material price fluctuations, labor shortages, and regulatory changes, so that they understand what could impact the budget down the line.

Provide Regular Updates

Keeping stakeholders updated on the real-time progress of the project—and any potential cost increases—is critical to maintaining trust. Rather than waiting until costs have already escalated, provide detailed regular budget and timeline updates, even if there are no changes. This proactive communication shows that you're on top of things and gives stakeholders a chance to weigh in before problems escalate.

Use Data to Support Your Case

When discussing cost escalations with stakeholders, data is your best friend. Use your detailed documentation to show exactly what has caused the increase and how it will impact the overall budget and timeline. This kind of transparency helps stakeholders see the situation more objectively and makes it easier for them to approve any necessary adjustments.

Creating a Contingency Plan

No matter how well you plan, some level of cost escalation is almost inevitable in a construction project. That's why having a solid contingency plan is so important. By planning for the unexpected, you can respond to cost increases quickly and minimize their impact.

Anticipate Common Risks

The first step in creating a contingency plan is identifying the most common risks to your project's budget. As mentioned earlier, material price fluctuations, labor shortages, and site conditions are some of the biggest culprits. By anticipating these risks and building them into your project's budget, you're already one step ahead when challenges arise.

Identify Cost-Saving Opportunities

When faced with cost escalations, it's important to have options for reducing costs elsewhere in the project. This might mean sourcing cheaper materials, adjusting the project's scope, or finding more efficient ways to use labor. Identifying these cost-saving opportunities in advance allows you to act quickly and keep the project on track, even if the budget takes a hit.

Regularly Revisit Your Contingency Plan

A contingency plan isn't something you create once and then forget about. It should be a living document that evolves as the project progresses. Regularly revisiting your contingency plan allows you to make adjustments based on new information and changing circumstances, ensuring that you're always prepared for whatever comes your way.

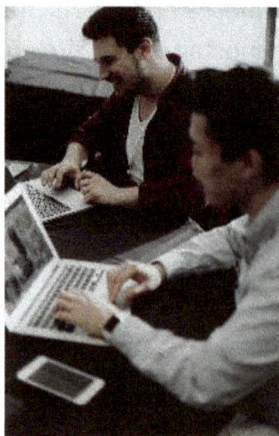

CHAPTER 5

Communicating Changes Effectively

Strategies for Internal Communication

The Importance of Clear Communication

Managing cost escalations isn't just about keeping the project on track —it's also about how you communicate these changes to the people who matter. Whether it's clients, investors, or team members, delivering bad news about rising costs can be tricky. But if done right, clear and timely communication can make all the difference between a manageable adjustment and a full-blown crisis.

Be Transparent and Direct

When it comes to communicating cost escalations, transparency is key. It's important to be upfront and direct about what's causing the increase, how much it will impact the budget, and what steps you're taking to mitigate the situation. Sugar-coating the issue or avoiding the conversation will only make things worse in the long run. Be honest about the challenges you're facing and provide as much detail as possible to explain the situation.

Timing Matters

The timing of your communication is just as important as what you say. The sooner you let stakeholders know about cost escalations, the better. Waiting until the last moment to deliver the news can catch people off guard and make the situation seem worse than it is. By providing updates early and often, you give stakeholders a chance to weigh in and offer solutions before the problem escalates.

Focus on Solutions, Not Just the Problem

No one likes hearing that a project is going over budget. But delivering bad news with a plan for how to fix it can make the situation much more manageable. When discussing cost increases with stakeholders, don't just present the problem—offer solutions. Whether it's adjusting the project scope, negotiating better rates with suppliers, or finding ways to save on labor, showing that you're actively working to control costs helps build trust and keeps the conversation productive.

Tailoring Your Message to Different Audiences

Not all stakeholders are going to respond to cost escalations in the same way. Each audience—whether it's clients, investors, or your internal team—will have different concerns, so it's important to tailor your message accordingly.

Clients: Keep the Focus on Value

When communicating cost increases to clients, it's essential to frame the conversation around value. Clients want to know that their investment is still worth it, even if the price has gone up. Emphasize the long-term benefits of the project and explain how the cost increase will contribute to delivering a high-quality result. For example, if material costs have risen, explain how using higher-quality materials will improve the project's durability or reduce maintenance costs down the line.

Investors: Show How You're Protecting Their Investment

Investors are likely to be more concerned about the financial implications of a cost increase, so it's important to focus on how you're mitigating risk. Provide a detailed breakdown of what caused the escalation, how much it will impact the overall budget, and what steps you're taking to minimize the financial impact. Use data and historical performance to back up your claims, showing that you have a track record of delivering projects successfully despite challenges.

Internal Teams: Keep the Morale High

Communicating cost escalations to your internal team can be tricky, especially if they feel responsible for keeping the project on budget. It's important that you approach each of these conversations with sincere empathy and be understanding, while also encouraging a problem-solving mindset. Focus on how the team can work together to seek out and find creative solutions and to keep the project moving forward. Acknowledge the hard work they've already put in and highlight the progress that's been made, so they stay motivated even in the face of challenges.

Managing Difficult Conversations

Cost escalations often lead to tough conversations, especially when clients or investors are frustrated by the additional expenses. Managing these discussions with professionalism and empathy is critical to maintaining strong relationships and keeping the project on track.

Stay Calm and Professional

When emotions are running high, it's easy to get defensive or feel overwhelmed. But keeping your cool and approaching the conversation calmly will help defuse the situation. Listen carefully to the concerns being raised, acknowledge any frustrations, and respond thoughtfully. By staying composed, you set the tone for a more productive discussion.

Empathy Goes a Long Way

It's important to remember that cost escalations don't just affect the project—they affect the people involved. Clients may be concerned about their own budget constraints, and your team might be feeling the pressure of meeting deadlines despite the challenges. Showing empathy and understanding the impact these escalations have on others can make a big difference in how your message is received.

Offer Alternatives

Whenever possible, provide alternatives or compromises to soften the impact of cost increases. Maybe the project scope can be adjusted to stay within budget, or perhaps payment terms can be renegotiated to ease the financial burden on clients. Offering solutions not only helps manage the situation but also shows that you're committed to finding a path forward that works for everyone.

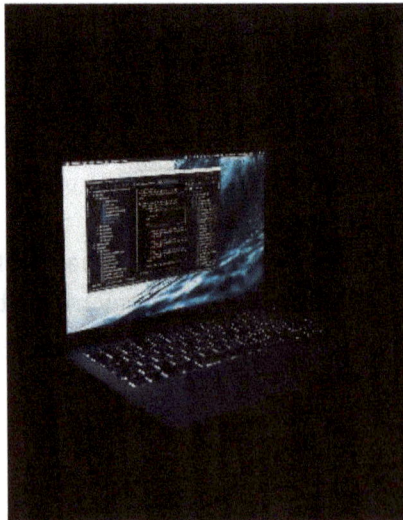

Documenting Cost Escalation Conversations

In construction, documentation isn't just for tracking expenses—it's also an essential part of communication, especially when it comes to cost escalations. Documenting conversations with stakeholders helps ensure that everyone is on the same page and protects you from potential disputes later on.

Keep Detailed Records of Discussions

Whether you're discussing cost increases with clients, investors, or subcontractors, it's important to keep detailed records of every conversation. Document the key points discussed, any decisions made, and any action items agreed upon. This documentation serves as a reference point if there's any confusion or disagreement down the road.

Use Written Confirmations

After having a verbal conversation about cost escalations, follow up with a written confirmation—such as an email or meeting minutes—that outlines what was discussed and what the next steps are. This creates a paper trail that could effectively be used to resolve any future disputes and helps keep everyone accountable for their responsibilities.

Maintain a Centralized Communication Log

Consider using a centralized communication log where all discussions about cost escalations are recorded and accessible to key stakeholders. This log ensures that everyone has access to the same information and can review past conversations if needed. It also provides transparency, which can help prevent misunderstandings and build trust.

Conclusion: How to Turn Cost Escalations into Opportunities

While cost escalations can be challenging, they also present an opportunity to demonstrate your expertise, creativity, and leadership. By handling cost increases with transparency, strategic planning, and clear communication, you not only keep your project on track—you strengthen your relationships with stakeholders and show your ability to manage complex projects with confidence.

When you approach cost escalations with a solution-oriented mindset, they become less of a roadblock and more of a chance to prove your value. Whether it's through better documentation, more strategic contract negotiations, or improved communication, each challenge gives you the opportunity to refine your process and improve future projects.

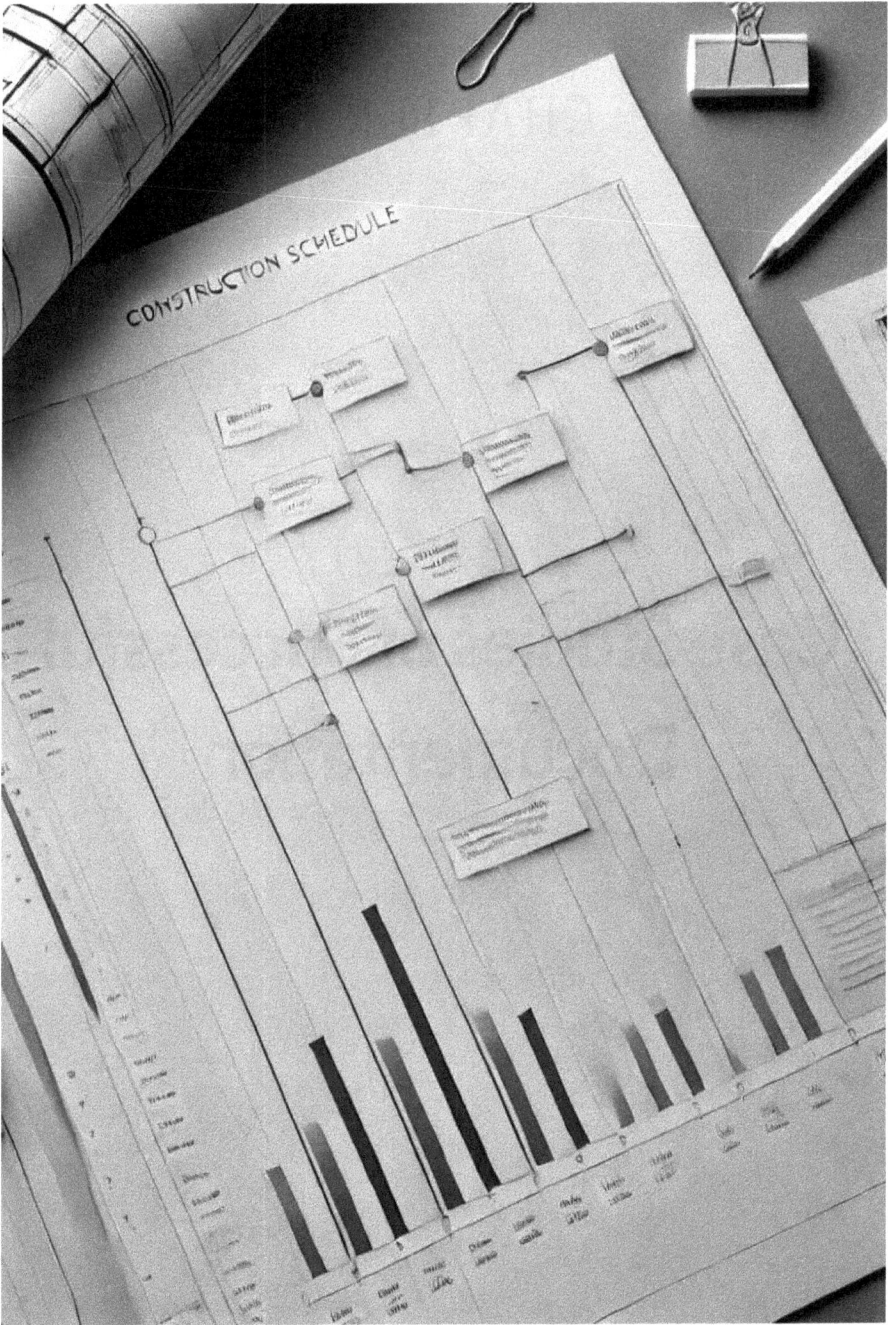

CHAPTER 6

Case Studies of Successful Documentation

Analyzing Successful Projects

The Role of Technology in Managing Cost Escalations

The construction industry has historically been slow to recognize and adopt new technologies, but times are changing. Today, the technology available plays a crucial role in helping project managers stay ahead of cost escalations. From real-time tracking to predictive analytics, modern tools allow you to make smarter decisions and catch potential issues before they spiral out of control.

Real-Time Cost Tracking

One of the largest advantages of using technology in construction is the ability to track costs in real time. With project management software, you can monitor expenses as they happen, rather than waiting until the end of the month to discover that you've gone over budget. These tools can alert you when costs are approaching your budget threshold, giving you the chance to take corrective action before things get out of hand.

Using Data to Make Better Predictions

Modern construction technology doesn't just help you manage current costs—it can also help predict future ones. With tools that analyze historical data and current trends, you can identify patterns that could lead to cost increases. For instance, if material prices tend to rise at certain times of the year, you can plan your purchases accordingly. These insights help you make informed decisions about everything from labor allocation to procurement, reducing the likelihood of budget surprises down the road.

Streamlining Communication and Collaboration

Technology also makes it easier to keep everyone on the same page. Cloud-based platforms allow you to store all project documents—like contracts, change orders, and budgets—in one place. This ensures that everyone involved needing access has real-time access to the latest information, whether they're in the office or out in the field. By centralizing your communication and documentation, you reduce the risk of miscommunication, which is a major cause of cost increases.

Tools That Help Control Costs

With so many tools available, it's important to choose the ones that best suit your individual project's needs. Here are a few types of technology that can help you manage cost escalations more effectively:

1. **Project Management Software**: These state of the are platforms allow you to track expenses, monitor timelines, and manage resources all in one place. Many of them offer real-time updates, which means you can catch cost overruns early and address them quickly.
2. **Cost Estimating Software**: When you're preparing bids, cost estimating software helps you generate more accurate estimates by factoring in current material prices, labor costs, and potential risks. This helps prevent underestimating, which is a common cause of cost escalation.
3. **Building Information Modeling (BIM)**: BIM software allows you to create accurate and precisely detailed 3D models of your project, making it easier to identify potential issues before construction even begins. By catching design flaws early, you can avoid costly changes later in the project.
4. **Drones and Site Monitoring**: Drones offer a way to monitor progress and site conditions in real time, providing a bird's-eye view of the entire project. Regular drone surveys can help identify issues early—like safety hazards or unexpected site conditions—allowing you to make adjustments before they affect your timeline and budget.
5. **Financial Management Software**: Financial software designed specifically for construction projects can help you manage cash flow, track invoices, and forecast future expenses. By staying on top of your finances, you reduce the costly risk of running out of funds mid-project.

How to Implement Technology Successfully

While technology offers plenty of benefits, the key to success is implementing it the right way. If your team isn't properly trained or the software isn't tailored to your specific needs, you might find yourself facing more problems than solutions.

Start with Clear Objectives

Before you invest in any new technology, it's important to identify your goals. Are you looking to reduce project delays, improve cost tracking, or enhance collaboration? Defining your objectives upfront will help you choose the right tools and ensure that your team is using them effectively.

Train Your Team

Introducing new technology can be a big adjustment, so it's crucial to provide thorough training. Make sure everyone—from project managers to field workers—understands how to use the new tools and why they're important. Providing ongoing team training and support will also help address any issues as they arise.

Choose Tools That Fit Your Project

Not all technology is a one-size-fits-all solution. It's important to choose the proper tools that are specifically designed for the construction industry and that fit the unique needs of your project. For example, smaller projects may benefit from simpler project management software, while larger, more complex projects might require advanced tools like BIM or financial forecasting software.

Evaluate and Adapt

Finally, remember that implementing new technology is an ongoing process. Regularly evaluate your tools and the effectiveness of them to make adjustments as needed. What works for one project might not work for the next, so be open to experimenting with different platforms and approaches until you find what works best for your team.

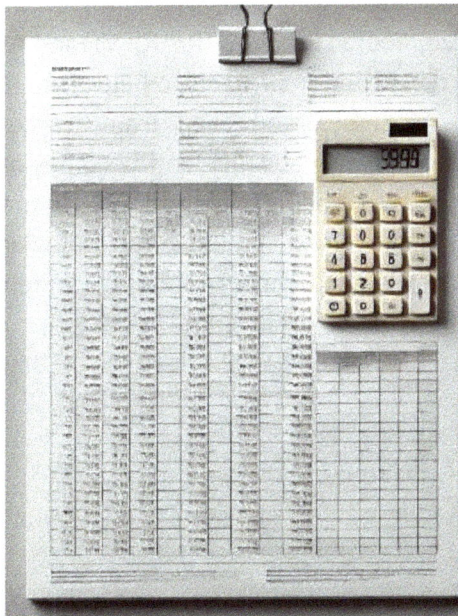

The Future of Technology in Construction

Technology in construction is advancing quickly, and the tools that are available today are just the beginning. As the industry continues to evolve, we can expect to see even more innovations aimed at improving cost management and reducing project delays. Here are a few trends to keep an eye on:

1. **Artificial Intelligence (AI)**: AI is making its way into construction, offering the potential to automate processes like cost estimating, scheduling, and even risk management. As AI becomes more available and sophisticated, it will allow project managers to make data-driven decisions faster and with greater accuracy.
2. **Robotics**: Robotics are being developed to handle repetitive tasks like bricklaying or pouring concrete, which could help reduce labor costs and improve efficiency. While still in the early stages, the integration of robotics into construction could have a major impact on how projects are executed.
3. **Virtual and Augmented Reality (VR/AR)**: VR and AR are already being used in some construction projects to help visualize designs, simulate construction processes, and even train workers. As this newer technology continues to advance and becomes more accessible, we can look forwards to it being widely adopted in the industry.
4. **Sustainability Tech**: Green building technologies, such as energy-efficient materials and smart building systems, are becoming increasingly popular. These innovations not only help reduce environmental impact but can also lead to cost savings over time.

Conclusion: Embracing Technology for Better Cost Control

The construction industry is entering a new era, where the use of new technology is no longer a choice of luxury but has become a necessity. By embracing these tools, you'll not only improve your ability to manage costs but also enhance the overall efficiency and success across your projects. The key is to choose the right tools for your specific needs, train your team thoroughly, and stay flexible as new innovations emerge. With the right technology in place, you'll be better equipped to handle cost escalations, stay within budget, and deliver projects that exceed client expectations.

CHAPTER 7

Navigating Regulatory Requirements

Understanding Federal Guidelines

Understanding the Role of Risk Management in Cost Control

Cost escalations don't just happen out of the blue—they are often the result of unanticipated risks that were not managed effectively. Whether it's material shortages, weather delays, or labor issues, risks in construction are inevitable. That's why having a solid risk management strategy in place is key to keeping your project on budget and avoiding costly surprises.

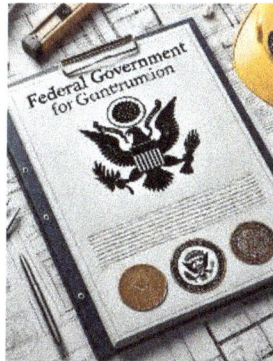

Risk management isn't about eliminating risk entirely (that's impossible in construction), but rather about anticipating potential issues and creating a plan to deal with them if they arise. By understanding the potential risks to your project and being proactive in addressing them, you can greatly reduce the likelihood of cost escalations.

Identifying Common Construction Risks

Every construction project is unique, but there are certain risks that tend to crop up more frequently. Let's take a look at some of the most common risks that can lead to cost escalations:

1. **Material Shortages**: Construction relies heavily on the availability of materials, and when there's a shortage—whether due to supply chain disruptions or increased demand—prices can skyrocket. Planning ahead and building strong relationships with suppliers can help you mitigate the impact of material shortages.
2. **Labor Shortages**: Skilled labor can be hard to come by, especially in times of high demand. A lack of available workers can cause delays, which ultimately drives up project costs. Investing in workforce development and retaining skilled workers can help avoid these issues.
3. **Weather-Related Delays**: Weather can be a major disruptor for construction projects. Heavy rain, snow, or extreme temperatures can all cause delays, leading to extended project timelines and additional costs. Having a weather contingency plan in place is essential for managing this risk.
4. **Design Changes**: When design changes are made after construction has started, it can lead to additional labor and material costs. These changes are often driven by client requests or unforeseen site conditions. Ensuring thorough design reviews before construction begins and setting clear expectations with clients can minimize the risk of costly changes.
5. **Regulatory Compliance**: Staying on top of building codes, safety regulations, and environmental standards is crucial to avoiding fines, delays, and extra costs. Make sure your team is well-versed in local and federal regulations to prevent compliance issues from causing cost escalations.

Creating a Risk Management Plan

Now that we've identified some common risks, let's talk about how to build a risk management plan that will help you stay on budget and avoid escalating costs. Here is a step-by-step guide to help you create an effective plan:

1. **Identify Potential Risks**: The first step in any risk management plan is identifying the risks that are most likely to affect your project. These could be related to materials, labor, weather, regulations, or any other factors that have the potential to disrupt your timeline or budget.

2. **Assess the Impact of Each Risk**: Once you've identified the risks, the next step is to assess how likely each one is to occur and how much impact it would have on the project. Some risks might be highly likely but have a minimal impact, while others could be less likely but have a significant effect on the budget if they do occur.

3. **Prioritize Risks**: After assessing the impact of each risk, you can prioritize them based on which ones are most critical to your project's success. Focusing on the highest-priority risks will help you allocate your resources more effectively.

4. **Develop Mitigation Strategies**: For each of your high-priority risks, you should create a plan for how you'll manage them if they occur. This could involve securing alternative suppliers, building contingency budgets, or creating buffer time in your schedule. The goal is to have a plan in place that allows you to respond quickly and minimize the impact on your project.

5. **Monitor and Adapt**: Risk management is an ongoing process, so it's important to regularly monitor the risks you've identified and adjust your plan as needed. New risks can emerge over the course of a project, so staying flexible and ready to adapt is key.

Mitigating Risk with Contingency Budgets

One of the best ways to manage risk in construction is by setting aside a contingency budget. A contingency budget acts as a financial buffer, allowing you to cover unexpected costs without jeopardizing the overall project budget. The key to an effective contingency budget is planning for the right amount—too little, and you won't have enough to cover cost increases; too much, and you could be tying up resources unnecessarily.

How Much Should You Allocate for Contingencies?

The amount you allocate for contingencies will depend on the complexity, intricacies, and scale of your project. For smaller, less complex projects, a contingency budget of around 5% of the total project cost is generally sufficient. However, for larger or more complex projects, you may need to set aside closer to 10–15% to account for the additional risks involved. It's important to revisit your contingency budget regularly as the project progresses, adjusting it as needed to reflect any new risks or changes.

When to Use the Contingency Budget

It's important to treat your contingency budget as a safety net, not as part of your regular project spending. Only dip into it when an unexpected cost arises that couldn't have been anticipated during the planning stage. Make sure to document every instance where you use contingency funds, so you can track how much is being spent and ensure you stay within the budgeted amount.

The Importance of Insurance in Risk Management

Another important element of risk management in construction is having the right insurance in place. Construction projects are vulnerable to a wide range of risks, from accidents on-site to damage caused by natural disasters. Having comprehensive insurance coverage ensures that you're protected from financial losses when things go wrong.

Types of Insurance to Consider

1. **General Liability Insurance**: This type of insurance covers accidents or injuries that occur on-site, protecting your business from costly lawsuits or claims.

2. **Builder's Risk Insurance**: Builder's risk insurance covers damage to the project itself, whether it's caused by fire, theft, or extreme weather. It's especially important for large projects with a high financial investment.

3. **Professional Liability Insurance**: Also known as errors and omissions insurance, this coverage typically protects you if a design flaw or mistake causes the project to go over budget or requires costly corrections.

4. **Workers' Compensation Insurance**: In many regions, workers' compensation insurance is required by law. It covers medical costs and lost wages for workers who are injured on the job.

Conclusion: Risk Management as a Path to Success

Effective risk management is one of the most powerful tools in your arsenal when it comes to controlling costs and delivering successful projects. By identifying potential risks early, creating contingency plans, and making sure you have the right insurance in place, you'll be well-prepared to handle whatever challenges come your way. Rather than viewing risks as obstacles, think of them as opportunities to demonstrate your ability to navigate complex projects with confidence and skill. In the end, a proactive approach to risk management not only protects your budget—it enhances your reputation as a leader in the construction industry.

CHAPTER 8

Training and Development for Project Teams

Importance of Training in Documentation

The Importance of Contracts in Cost Management

Contracts are necessary for any successful construction project. They set the expectations for how the work will be completed, how much it will cost, and what happens if things do not go as planned. When managing cost escalations, the terms of the contract can make all the difference. A well-structured contract protects the company's financial interests and provides the flexibility to adapt to unexpected price increases or project changes.

By including the right clauses in your contracts, you can reduce the risk of disputes, manage cost escalations more effectively, and ensure that the company and the clients are on the same page regarding how budget changes will be handled.

Key Clauses to Include in Your Contracts

Here are some of the most important clauses to consider when drafting a contract to manage cost escalations:

1. **Escalation Clauses**: One of the best ways to protect the company from rising material or labor costs is by including an escalation clause in the contract. This clause allows for price adjustments based on market fluctuations. For example, if the steel price increases by over a certain percentage, the client agrees to cover the additional cost. Escalation clauses should reference an objective cost index, like the Producer Price Index (PPI) or other Material Cost Index (MCI, to ensure fairness for both parties.

2. **Force Majeure Clauses**: Sometimes, events beyond anyone's control—like natural disasters, pandemics, or political unrest—cause delays or increase costs. A force majeure clause protects the company by excusing delays or allowing for cost adjustments in these situations. Without this clause, the company could bear the brunt of unforeseen costs that were out of their control.

3. **Scope Change Clauses**: Clients often request changes to the original project scope, which can lead to higher material and labor costs. A scope change clause ensures that any changes requested after starting the project are well documented and priced accordingly. This clause protects the company from absorbing the extra costs associated with scope creep and ensures clients know the financial impact of any requests.

4. **Payment Terms**: Clear payment terms are essential for managing cash flow and ensuring that the company gets paid promptly when cost escalations occur. The contract should outline when payments are due, how they will be made, and what happens if payments are delayed. Including provisions for progress payments or milestone-based payments can help ensure that the company receives regular payments as the project progresses.

5. **Dispute Resolution Clauses**: Disputes are inevitable in construction, especially when it comes to cost increases. A dispute resolution clause outlines how disagreements will be handled through negotiation, mediation, or arbitration. Having this process spelled out in the contract can prevent costly and time-consuming legal battles during or after the project.

Negotiating Contracts with Flexibility in Mind

When drafting or negotiating contracts, it's important to attain a balance between protecting the company's interests and maintaining flexibility. Project Managers should want to ensure that the company is covered in case of cost escalations, but they also need to be realistic about the client's concerns and expectations.

Be Clear About Price Adjustments

One of the most important things to discuss during contract negotiations is how price adjustments will processed. Be upfront with the client about possible cost increases due to factors including market volatility and supply chain disruptions. Setting clear expectations from the beginning will reduce the likelihood of disputes later on.

Offer Solutions for Managing Costs

During contract negotiations, it can be helpful to offer solutions that benefit both parties. For example, the contractor could suggest locking in material prices early or establishing long-term supplier agreements to mitigate the risk of price increases. Offering alternatives shows that the contractor is proactive and committed to keeping costs under control, which can help build trust with the client.

Fixed-Price vs. Cost-Plus Contracts

One of the biggest decisions that must be made when negotiating contracts is whether to use a fixed-price or cost-plus structure. Both have pros and cons, especially when it comes to managing cost escalations.

Fixed-Price Contracts

With a fixed-price contract, the contractor agrees to complete the project for a set price, regardless of how much it costs the company. This type of contract appeals to clients because it provides them with a clear budget. However, fixed-price contracts can be risky if material prices or labor costs increase unexpectedly. In a proactive approach to help mitigate risk, it is vital to include escalation clauses or to pad the initial estimate with a contingency buffer.

Cost-Plus Contracts

A cost-plus contract, on the other hand, allows the contractor to be reimbursed for the project's actual costs plus an agreed-upon fee (either a fixed amount or a percentage of the costs). This type of contract is more flexible and typically reduces the risk of losing money due to cost escalations, but it can make clients nervous because they have less certainty about the final cost. To make a cost-plus contract more appealing to clients, a contractor can offer to set a cap on the total project cost or provide regular budget updates.

Managing Client Expectations Through Contractual Terms

One of the best ways to manage client expectations is by clearly outlining how cost escalations will be processed in the contract. Clients may be concerned about rising costs, but if they understand upfront how price adjustments will be managed, it helps build trust and prevent misunderstandings later on.

Communicate Early and Often

When first discussing the contract with the client, communicate the potential for cost escalations and explain how the company accounted for those risks in the contract. Be transparent about what factors could lead to increased costs and how those costs will be calculated. Setting these expectations early on helps clients feel more in control and reassures them that a plan is in place.

Build Flexibility Into the Timeline

Cost escalations often lead to delays, which can frustrate clients and put pressure on project deadlines. To manage this, include flexible language in the contract regarding the project timeline. Allow for extensions if certain events—like material shortages or labor strikes—delay the project. By building flexibility into the timeline, the company is protected from penalties and helps manage client expectations if things don't go as planned.

The Importance of Regular Contract Reviews

A contract should not be signed and forgotten about. It's a living document that should be reviewed regularly throughout the project to ensure that both parties are meeting their obligations and that any changes are properly documented.

Schedule Regular Check-Ins

Scheduling regular check-ins with the client to review the contract can help catch potential issues early and ensure that both parties are on the same page. These check-ins are also an excellent opportunity to discuss upcoming risks that could affect the budget or timeline, allowing the contractor make adjustments before they become bigger problems.

Document Every Change

Every change to the project, no matter how small, should be documented and attached to the contract as an amendment. This includes change orders, timeline extensions, or price adjustments. By keeping the contract up to date, you protect yourself from disputes later on and ensure that everyone understands the current terms of the agreement.

Conclusion: Contracts as a Tool for Controlling Costs

At the end of the day, your contract is one of the most powerful tools you have for managing cost escalations. By including the right clauses, setting clear expectations, and maintaining flexibility, you can protect your financial interests and keep your project on track. A well-drafted contract not only helps you navigate the complexities of construction but also strengthens your relationships with clients by providing transparency and trust. When both parties are aligned on how cost escalations will be handled, it creates a smoother, more successful project from start to finish.

CHAPTER 9

Future Trends in Cost Documentation

Emerging Technologies in the Construction Industry

Why Strong Leadership Matters

In construction, managing cost escalations is about more than just numbers—it's about how well you lead your team and guide the project through challenges. Strong leadership plays a critical role in keeping costs under control, especially when unexpected problems arise. A capable leader is able to make tough decisions, maintain team morale, and communicate effectively with clients and stakeholders, all while steering the project toward successful completion.

Good leaders don't just react to cost escalations—they anticipate them. By fostering a culture of proactive problem-solving and open communication, you can prevent small issues from snowballing into larger, more costly problems.

Setting the Tone from Day One

As a leader, your approach to managing costs sets the tone for the entire project. From the very first meeting, it's important to emphasize the importance of staying on budget and being mindful of potential cost escalations. This not only sets clear expectations for your team but also helps ensure that everyone is working toward the same financial goals.

Establish Clear Roles and Responsibilities

One of the first steps in managing cost escalations effectively is to establish clear roles and responsibilities for everyone involved. Who is responsible for tracking costs? Who will report any changes or potential risks? By assigning these roles early on, you ensure that nothing slips through the cracks and that everyone is accountable for their part in managing the project's budget.

Encourage Open Communication

Cost issues are often made worse when there's a breakdown in communication. It's essential for managers to foster an environment where team members feel comfortable bringing up concerns, whether it's about budget issues, potential delays, or design changes. When people are afraid to speak up, small problems can quickly turn into major cost escalations. As a leader, it's your job to encourage open and honest communication so that issues are addressed early and effectively.

Decision-Making Under Pressure

In the fast-paced world of construction, leaders are constantly faced with tough decisions—especially when cost escalations threaten to derail a project. Making smart, timely decisions under pressure is one of the most important skills a leader can have.

Evaluate the Situation Thoroughly

Before making a decision, it's crucial to gather as much information as possible. What's causing the cost increase? Are there any alternative solutions? How will this decision affect the overall timeline and budget? By evaluating the situation thoroughly, you can make informed decisions that balance cost control with project progress.

Know When to Take Action

That said, it's also important to know when to act. In construction, time is money, and waiting too long to make a decision can quickly result in even greater cost increases. As a leader, you need to trust your judgment and act decisively, when necessary, while still weighing the potential impact of each choice.

Lead with Confidence

When cost escalations happen, it's easy for a project to lose momentum or for team members to become discouraged. As a leader, your confidence is key to keeping everyone motivated and focused. Even when facing budget challenges, maintaining a positive and solution-oriented attitude helps your team stay engaged and committed to finding ways to control costs and keep the project moving forward.

Empowering Your Team to Manage Costs

Great leaders know that they can't do everything alone. Empowering your team to take ownership of cost management is essential to staying within budget. By giving your team the tools, authority, and autonomy they need to make decisions, you create a sense of responsibility and accountability across the entire project.

Provide the Right Tools

Cost management can be complex, especially on large projects with multiple moving parts. Make sure your team has access to the right tools and technology to track expenses, manage resources, and forecast potential risks. Project management software, cost tracking tools, and regular budget updates all help your team stay on top of costs.

Encourage Problem-Solving

When cost escalations occur, it's easy to fall into the trap of pointing fingers or blaming external factors. But successful leaders create a culture of problem-solving, where the focus is on finding solutions, not assigning blame. Encourage your team to think creatively about how to address cost increases, whether it's by adjusting the project scope, finding alternative materials, or reallocating resources.

Recognize and Reward Cost-Conscious Behavior

One of the most effective ways to foster a cost-conscious culture is to recognize and reward team members who take steps to manage costs. Whether it's identifying potential savings or successfully negotiating with a supplier, acknowledging these efforts shows your team that cost control is a priority and encourages them to continue finding ways to stay within budget.

Communicating with Stakeholders

Leadership isn't just about managing your internal team—it's also about maintaining strong relationships with clients, investors, and other stakeholders. When cost escalations occur, clear and transparent communication with stakeholders is essential for maintaining trust and keeping the project on track.

Be Transparent About Cost Increases

No one likes to hear that a project is going over budget, but keeping stakeholders in the dark will only lead to frustration and distrust. As soon as you become aware of a potential cost escalation, communicate it clearly and honestly with your stakeholders. Explain the cause of the increase, how it will affect the overall budget, and what steps you're taking to mitigate the impact.

Present Solutions, Not Just Problems

When discussing cost increases with stakeholders, it's important to frame the conversation around solutions. Rather than simply presenting the problem, explain what actions you're taking to keep costs under control and prevent further escalations. Whether it's adjusting the timeline, renegotiating contracts, or finding alternative materials, offering solutions shows that you're actively managing the situation and gives stakeholders confidence in your leadership.

Maintain Regular Updates

Cost escalations are less likely to cause tension if stakeholders feel informed and involved throughout the project. By providing regular updates on the budget, timeline, and potential risks, you keep stakeholders in the loop and prevent surprises. This proactive communication helps build trust and ensures that stakeholders are prepared if and when cost increases occur.

Building a Resilient Team

Cost escalations can put a strain on even the most experienced teams, so it's important to build resilience into your project's culture. A resilient team has ability to adapt to challenges, stay focused under pressure, and continue delivering high-quality work despite setbacks.

Foster a Collaborative Environment

Collaboration is key to managing cost escalations effectively. Encourage your team to work together to find solutions and overcome obstacles. By fostering a collaborative environment, you create a culture where everyone feels responsible for the project's success and is willing to contribute their ideas and expertise to manage costs.

Promote Flexibility and Adaptability

In construction, things rarely go according to plan. A resilient team is disciplined and can adapt to changing circumstances without losing focus. As a leader, it's important to promote flexibility and adaptability, encouraging your team to stay open to new ideas and approaches when faced with cost increases.

Celebrate Successes

Managing a construction project—especially one with cost escalations—is no easy feat. Take the time to celebrate your team's successes, whether it's hitting a budget milestone or finding a creative solution to a cost increase. Recognizing these achievements helps keep morale high and reinforces the importance of teamwork and problem-solving.

Conclusion: Leading Through Cost Escalations

Cost escalations are an inevitable part of construction, but with strong leadership, they don't have to derail your project. By setting clear expectations, empowering your team, and maintaining open communication with stakeholders, you can navigate these challenges with confidence. Great leaders don't just manage costs—they inspire project teams to rise up to the occasion and deliver successful projects despite the obstacles faced.

In the end, leadership is about more than just controlling the budget—it's about guiding your team through tough situations, making smart decisions under pressure, and building a resilient, solution-oriented culture. When you lead with clarity, confidence, and collaboration, cost escalations become just another challenge to overcome on the path to a successful project.

CHAPTER 10

Conclusion and Action Plan

Summary of Key Strategies

The Power of Learning from Experience

When it comes to managing cost escalations in construction, there's no better teacher than experience. By analyzing real-life projects, we can see firsthand how different strategies either succeeded or failed when faced with rising costs. These case studies provide valuable insights into how to anticipate and respond to challenges, helping you make smarter decisions on future projects.

In this chapter, we'll explore several real-world examples of cost escalations in construction. From large-scale infrastructure projects to smaller residential builds, we'll examine the common pitfalls that lead to budget overruns and highlight the strategies that successful teams used to bring their projects back on track.

Case Study 1: Managing Material Price Fluctuations in a High-Risk Market

The Challenge:

In 2021, a mid-sized construction firm was hired to complete a commercial building project in a rapidly growing urban area. While the project was initially budgeted at $5 million, the price of key materials like steel and lumber skyrocketed due to supply chain disruptions and increased global demand. Within months, material costs had risen by 20%, pushing the project significantly over budget.

What Went Wrong:

The project's original contract didn't include an escalation clause, leaving the contractor to absorb the rising material costs. Additionally, the team didn't anticipate how volatile the market would be and had not locked in material prices early on. By the time the cost increases were noticed, the project was already underway, and options for controlling costs were limited.

The Solution:

The construction firm quickly shifted gears by renegotiating with suppliers and securing bulk purchases of materials at a fixed price to prevent further increases. They also worked with the client to adjust the project's timeline, allowing them to complete certain phases while waiting for material prices to stabilize. To offset the rising costs, the team found ways to reduce labor hours through more efficient scheduling and streamlined workflows.

Key Takeaways:

- Always include an escalation clause in contracts to protect against unexpected price increases.
- Lock in material prices as early as possible, especially when working in volatile markets.
- Flexibility in scheduling and efficient use of labor can help offset rising material costs.

Case Study 2: Navigating Labor Shortages on a Large Infrastructure Project

The Challenge:

A major highway expansion project faced significant delays when a labor shortage hit the construction industry in the region. As the demand for trade workers outpaced supply, wages rose sharply, driving up the project's labor costs by 15%. With a tight deadline and limited budget, the project team was under pressure to find a solution quickly.

What Went Wrong:

While the project's initial planning had accounted for labor costs, it didn't factor in the possibility of a labor shortage. The team also hadn't invested in workforce development, relying on the availability of external contractors rather than building a more robust in-house team.

The Solution:

The project managers took a proactive approach to the labor shortage by offering incentives to attract skilled workers, such as signing bonuses and flexible working hours. They also invested in training programs to upskill existing staff, reducing their reliance on outside contractors. By improving scheduling efficiency and breaking the project into smaller, more manageable phases, they were able to reduce the overall labor hours required to complete the work.

Key Takeaways:

- Always consider the potential for labor shortages in your risk assessments.
- Invest in workforce development and training to reduce reliance on external labor.
- Flexible scheduling and breaking projects into smaller phases can help manage labor constraints.

Case Study 3: Dealing with Design Changes on a Residential Development

The Challenge:

A construction firm was hired to build a luxury residential development, but halfway through the project, the client requested several design changes, including the addition of custom finishes and new amenities. These changes added complexity to the project, increased material and labor costs, and extended the timeline by several months.

What Went Wrong:

The original contract didn't include clear guidelines for handling design changes, leading to confusion and delays. The project team was also slow to communicate the cost implications of the changes to the client, which caused friction and led to disputes over who would cover the additional expenses.

The Solution:

The project managers quickly implemented a robust change order process to handle future design requests. They also renegotiated the contract with the client to include an updated budget and timeline that accounted for the new changes. To prevent further delays, the team worked closely with suppliers to expedite material deliveries and adjusted the project's schedule to allow for overlapping work on different phases.

Key Takeaways:

- Always include clear guidelines for handling design changes in the contract.
- Communicate the cost and timeline implications of changes to clients immediately.
- Implement a formal change order process to streamline future requests.

Case Study 4: Responding to Regulatory Changes in a Government Contract

The Challenge:

A government contractor working on a public building project was hit with unexpected regulatory changes mid-project. New environmental regulations required modifications to the building's design and materials, increasing the overall project costs by 10%. The contractor had not anticipated these changes and was unsure how to navigate the new requirements without going over budget.

What Went Wrong:

The project's initial risk assessment didn't fully account for potential regulatory changes. Additionally, the contractor was slow to engage with regulatory agencies, leading to further delays and cost escalations as they scrambled to comply with the new rules.

The Solution:

The contractor immediately reached out to regulatory agencies to clarify the new requirements and ensure that no further changes would be required. They also worked with the client to renegotiate the project's budget and timeline, accounting for the increased costs. To manage the additional expenses, the contractor identified areas where costs could be reduced, such as sourcing alternative materials that still met the new regulations.

Key Takeaways:

- Always factor potential regulatory changes into your risk assessments, especially for government contracts.
- Engage with regulatory agencies early and often to stay ahead of potential changes.
- Renegotiate contracts with clients when regulatory changes lead to unavoidable cost increases.

Case Study 5: Successful Use of Technology to Manage Cost Escalations

The Challenge:

A construction company was working on a high-rise office building when they encountered several unexpected issues, including design flaws, weather delays, and rising material prices. Without a clear plan in place, costs began to spiral out of control, and the project was at risk of missing its completion deadline.

What Went Right:

Rather than letting the project continue to fall behind, the company turned to construction management software to get a better handle on costs. The software allowed them to track expenses in real time, identify cost-saving opportunities, and make data-driven decisions about how to proceed. They also used Building Information Modeling (BIM) to address design issues early on, preventing more costly changes down the line.

The Solution:

By leveraging technology, the project team was able to gain a clearer understanding of where costs were escalating and take immediate action. They adjusted their schedule to reduce labor hours, locked in material prices with suppliers, and improved communication with stakeholders through regular progress updates. The project ultimately came in under budget and was completed on time, despite the initial setbacks.

Key Takeaways:

- Real-time cost tracking and data-driven decision-making are essential for managing cost escalations.
- Using technology like BIM can help identify and resolve design issues early, reducing future costs.
- Transparent communication with stakeholders is key to managing expectations and avoiding delays.

Conclusion: Learning from the Successes and Failures of Others

These case studies highlight both the challenges and solutions involved in managing cost escalations in construction. By learning from the successes and mistakes of others, you can apply these lessons to your own projects, improving your ability to anticipate and respond to cost increases. Whether it's negotiating better contracts, investing in technology, or fostering better communication, each of these strategies can help you deliver projects on time and within budget, no matter the obstacles.

CHAPTER 11

Best Practices for Long-Term Cost Management

Why Long-Term Cost Management Matters

In construction, managing costs isn't just about staying within the budget on a single project—it's about developing long-term strategies that set you up for success in future projects as well. While short-term cost control is essential, building a foundation for long-term cost management ensures that your business remains competitive and profitable over time. This chapter explores the best practices that will help you develop a long-term approach to managing costs effectively, from forecasting and budgeting to building strong relationships with suppliers and clients.

Developing a Long-Term Budgeting Strategy

One of the keys to long-term success in construction is learning how to create accurate, flexible budgets that can adapt to changing market conditions. A solid budgeting strategy is essential for keeping costs under control, not just during individual projects but across your entire portfolio.

Forecasting Costs Based on Historical Data

When developing your budgets, it's important to look at historical data to identify trends and patterns in cost escalation. By analyzing past projects, you can get a better understanding of the factors that typically lead to budget overruns, such as rising material prices, labor shortages, or regulatory changes. This allows you to create more accurate forecasts and build contingency plans into your budget.

Building Flexibility into Your Budget

No matter how well you plan, unexpected cost increases are always a possibility. That's why it's important to build flexibility into your budget. Set aside contingency funds to cover unforeseen expenses, and regularly review your budget to make adjustments as needed. A flexible budget allows you to respond to changes quickly, minimizing the impact on your project's overall costs.

Investing in Technology for Cost Control

As we discussed in earlier chapters, technology is one of the most powerful tools for managing costs in construction. But to see long-term benefits, it's important to invest in the right technologies and integrate them into your overall business strategy.

Using Predictive Analytics to Forecast Costs

Predictive analytics tools use data to forecast future costs, helping you anticipate potential cost increases and plan accordingly. By analyzing factors like material prices, labor trends, and market conditions, these tools can help you create more accurate budgets and identify areas where cost-saving measures can be implemented.

Leveraging Automation for Efficiency

Automation can help reduce costs by streamlining processes, reducing errors, and improving efficiency. From automated scheduling and cost tracking to procurement and reporting, these tools free up your team to focus on more strategic tasks while minimizing the risk of costly mistakes. Over time, investing in automation can lead to significant savings and improved project outcomes.

Building Strong Relationships with Suppliers

Your relationships with suppliers play a crucial role in long-term cost management. By building strong, mutually beneficial partnerships, you can secure better pricing, improve communication, and ensure that you have access to the materials you need when you need them.

Negotiate Long-Term Contracts

Whenever possible, negotiate long-term contracts with suppliers to lock in prices and protect yourself from market fluctuations. These agreements provide stability for both parties, allowing you to plan your budgets more effectively. Suppliers may also offer discounts or better terms in exchange for the guarantee of consistent business over time.

Maintain Open Communication

Good communication with suppliers is essential for avoiding misunderstandings and delays that can lead to cost increases. Keep your suppliers informed about your project timelines and any changes in your material needs. In turn, they'll be better equipped to provide you with timely deliveries and help you stay on budget.

Foster a Collaborative Relationship

Think of your suppliers as partners, not just vendors. By working together to solve problems—whether it's finding alternative materials or adjusting delivery schedules—you can create a more collaborative relationship that benefits both parties. This approach can help you secure more favorable terms and build trust, which is key to long-term success.

Strengthening Client Relationships for Long-Term Success

Your relationships with clients are just as important as your relationships with suppliers when it comes to managing costs over the long term. Happy, satisfied clients are more likely to return for future projects, refer new business, and be flexible when cost increases are unavoidable.

Set Clear Expectations from the Start

From the very first conversation with a client, it's important to set clear expectations about the potential for cost escalations. Be transparent about what factors could lead to price increases, such as changes in material costs, labor shortages, or scope changes. When clients understand these risks upfront, they're more likely to be cooperative when issues arise.

Communicate Regularly

Regular communication is key to maintaining strong client relationships and managing costs. Provide frequent updates on the project's budget, timeline, and any potential risks. When clients feel informed and involved, they're less likely to be surprised or frustrated if cost increases occur. This proactive approach helps build trust and keeps the project moving forward smoothly.

Offer Value Beyond the Project

To build long-term relationships with clients, it's important to offer value beyond just completing the project on time and within budget. This could include offering advice on future projects, helping them navigate regulatory requirements, or identifying cost-saving opportunities. By positioning yourself as a trusted partner, you increase the likelihood of repeat business and referrals, both of which are essential for long-term success.

Fostering a Culture of Cost Awareness in Your Team

Long-term cost management isn't just about budgeting and forecasting—it's also about creating a company culture where cost awareness is a priority. When everyone on your team understands the importance of managing costs, it becomes easier to control expenses and deliver successful projects consistently.

Provide Ongoing Training

Make sure your team is well-trained in cost management practices, including how to track expenses, identify potential risks, and find cost-saving opportunities. Providing ongoing training helps keep everyone up to date on the latest strategies and technologies for controlling costs, and it reinforces the importance of staying within budget.

Encourage Accountability

Create a culture where everyone feels responsible for managing costs, not just the project managers or finance team. Encourage team members to take ownership of their roles in controlling expenses, whether it's by managing labor hours more efficiently, finding ways to reduce material waste, or negotiating better terms with subcontractors.

Recognize and Reward Cost-Conscious Behavior

One of the best ways to promote a cost-conscious culture is by recognizing and rewarding team members who actively work to control costs. Whether it's identifying potential savings or coming up with creative solutions to cost escalations, acknowledging these efforts reinforces the importance of cost management and encourages others to do the same.

Continuously Improving Your Cost Management Processes

Long-term success in cost management requires continuous improvement. The construction industry is constantly evolving, and the strategies that worked on one project may not be as effective on the next. That's why it's important to regularly review your cost management processes and look for ways to improve them.

Conduct Post-Project Reviews

After each project, conduct a thorough review of how costs were managed. What worked well? What could have been done better? By analyzing the successes and challenges of each project, you can identify areas where improvements can be made and apply those lessons to future projects.

Stay Informed About Industry Trends

Staying up to date on industry trends, new technologies, and market conditions is essential for long-term cost management. Attend industry conferences, read relevant publications, and network with other professionals to keep your knowledge current. This allows you to anticipate changes and adjust your strategies accordingly.

Be Willing to Adapt

Flexibility is key to long-term success in cost management. What worked in the past might not work in the future, and the ability to adapt to new challenges is crucial. Whether it's adopting new technology, revising your budgeting process, or renegotiating contracts, staying open to change will help you stay competitive in the long run.

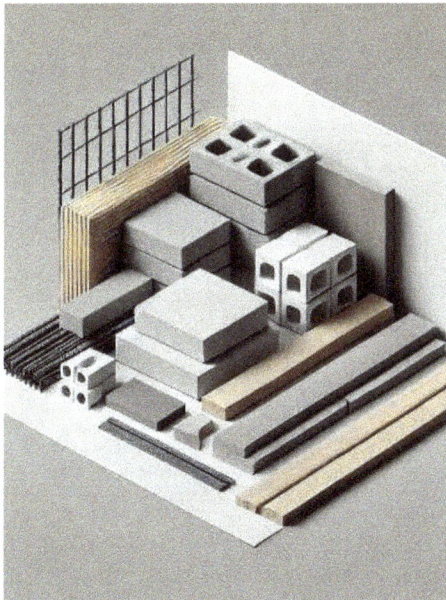

Conclusion: Building a Sustainable Cost Management Strategy

Effective cost management isn't just about finishing a project within budget—it's about developing a long-term strategy that allows you to grow, thrive, and stay competitive in a constantly changing industry. By investing in technology, building strong relationships, fostering a culture of cost awareness, and continuously improving your processes, you can create a sustainable approach to managing costs that will set you up for success on every project.

Remember, long-term success in construction requires more than just managing costs today—it's about planning for tomorrow and positioning yourself to handle whatever challenges come your way. With the right strategies in place, you can deliver projects that are not only on time and within budget but also set the foundation for lasting success.

CHAPTER 12

Future Trends in Construction Cost Management

The Evolving Landscape of Construction Costs

The construction industry is constantly changing, and with it comes new challenges and opportunities for managing costs. Staying ahead of these changes is key to long-term success. In this chapter, we'll explore some of the future trends that are expected to shape construction cost management, from technological advancements to shifting economic conditions. By understanding these trends, you can position yourself to stay competitive, adapt to new demands, and continue delivering projects efficiently and profitably.

Embracing Digital Transformation in Construction

Digital transformation is revolutionizing the construction industry, and it's having a profound impact on cost management. As more companies adopt digital tools, the ability to track, forecast, and control costs is becoming faster, more accurate, and more accessible.

Building Information Modeling (BIM) Becomes the Norm

BIM has already transformed the way construction projects are planned and executed, and its influence on cost management is only growing. As BIM technology continues to evolve, it allows for more precise cost estimation, better visualization of project changes, and improved collaboration among stakeholders. By integrating BIM with real-time cost tracking systems, project managers can gain a clearer picture of how design changes impact costs, leading to more informed decision-making and fewer budget overruns.

AI and Machine Learning for Predictive Cost Management

Artificial intelligence (AI) and machine learning are becoming increasingly important tools for predicting cost escalations before they happen. These technologies analyze vast amounts of data to identify patterns and trends, such as when certain materials are likely to increase in price or when labor shortages are expected to occur. By leveraging these insights, project managers can adjust their strategies proactively, helping to minimize cost overruns and improve budget accuracy.

Automation and Robotics to Reduce Labor Costs

The labor market in construction remains volatile, with ongoing shortages of skilled workers driving up wages. Automation and robotics offer a solution to these challenges by performing repetitive tasks such as bricklaying, concrete pouring, and even site inspections. While the upfront investment in robotics can be significant, the long-term savings in labor costs and increased efficiency make it an attractive option for many construction firms.

Sustainability and Green Building: The Cost of Going Green

As environmental concerns become more pressing, the demand for sustainable construction practices is on the rise. Green building initiatives not only reduce the environmental impact of construction projects but also present new challenges and opportunities for managing costs.

The Rising Demand for Sustainable Materials

The use of sustainable materials like recycled steel, energy-efficient insulation, and low-emission concrete is becoming more common, but these materials often come with higher upfront costs. As the market for green building continues to grow, prices are expected to stabilize, but for now, managing the cost of these materials requires careful planning. Project managers will need to balance the desire for sustainability with the realities of the budget, potentially by exploring incentives such as tax breaks or grants that can offset the additional costs of going green.

Energy-Efficient Buildings and Long-Term Savings

While sustainable construction practices can increase upfront costs, they often lead to long-term savings for building owners. Energy-efficient designs, smart building technologies, and renewable energy sources can reduce operational costs over time. As a result, project managers may find it easier to justify higher initial costs by demonstrating the long-term financial benefits to clients.

Modular Construction and Prefabrication: Faster Builds, Lower Costs

Modular construction and prefabrication are gaining traction as efficient and cost-effective alternatives to traditional building methods. These approaches involve constructing building components off-site and then assembling them on-site, reducing labor costs and construction time.

Faster Project Completion

One of the biggest advantages of modular construction is the ability to complete projects more quickly. With much of the work done off-site in controlled environments, weather delays and on-site disruptions are minimized. This faster turnaround can lead to significant cost savings, especially on projects with tight deadlines.

Reduced Material Waste

Prefabrication allows for more precise control over the amount of materials used, reducing waste and lowering overall material costs. By standardizing components and cutting materials to exact specifications, modular construction minimizes the likelihood of over-ordering and under-utilization, helping to keep projects within budget.

Flexibility and Scalability

Modular construction is also highly flexible, allowing for scalable designs that can be adapted to meet changing needs. This flexibility is especially valuable in projects where future expansion or modification is expected. By incorporating modular elements into the initial design, project managers can create more adaptable spaces without significantly increasing costs.

Supply Chain Resilience: Navigating Global Disruptions

The COVID-19 pandemic exposed the vulnerabilities in global supply chains, and construction was no exception. Disruptions to the availability of materials, delays in shipping, and rising transportation costs all had a significant impact on project budgets. As the world continues to recover, supply chain resilience has become a top priority for construction firms looking to manage costs more effectively.

Diversifying Supply Chains

One way to build supply chain resilience is by diversifying suppliers. Relying on a single supplier for key materials can leave projects vulnerable to disruptions, but by establishing relationships with multiple suppliers, project managers can mitigate the risk of shortages and price fluctuations. This approach also allows for more competitive pricing, as firms can negotiate better terms with a broader pool of vendors.

Localizing Material Sourcing

Sourcing materials locally can also help reduce the risks associated with global supply chain disruptions. While local materials may sometimes come at a premium, the reduction in transportation costs and the ability to avoid international shipping delays can make up for the difference. Additionally, local sourcing can contribute to sustainability goals by reducing the carbon footprint associated with long-distance shipping.

The Impact of Inflation and Interest Rates on Construction Costs

Inflation and fluctuating interest rates are ongoing challenges that will continue to affect construction costs in the coming years. As project managers look for ways to navigate these economic pressures, a deeper understanding of how inflation impacts material prices, labor costs, and financing is essential.

Managing the Rising Costs of Materials

Inflation can cause the prices of construction materials to rise significantly, straining project budgets. Project managers will need to adopt strategies such as bulk purchasing, long-term supplier contracts, and price-lock agreements to mitigate the impact of inflation on material costs. By anticipating price increases and planning accordingly, firms can protect their budgets from unexpected spikes.

Interest Rates and Financing Costs

Rising interest rates can increase the cost of borrowing for construction projects, affecting both the developer and the client. As financing becomes more expensive, project managers may need to explore alternative financing options, such as public-private partnerships (PPPs) or joint ventures, to share the financial burden and reduce the impact of interest rate hikes on the overall project budget.

Collaboration and Transparency: The Future of Client Relationships

As construction projects become more complex and the cost pressures increase, collaboration and transparency between project managers, clients, and stakeholders will be critical to success. The future of cost management lies in fostering strong, transparent relationships that allow for open communication, shared decision-making, and a collaborative approach to problem-solving.

Adopting Integrated Project Delivery (IPD)

Integrated Project Delivery (IPD) is a collaborative approach to construction that brings all stakeholders together early in the planning process. By aligning the interests of the client, contractor, and design team from the outset, IPD reduces the likelihood of disputes and cost overruns. This model encourages transparency and shared responsibility, leading to better cost management throughout the project lifecycle.

Open Book Accounting

Open book accounting is another trend gaining traction in the construction industry. This approach involves sharing all project-related financial information with the client, creating transparency and building trust. By allowing clients to see exactly where their money is going, project managers can foster more collaborative relationships and reduce the likelihood of disputes over cost escalations.

Conclusion: Preparing for the Future of Construction Cost Management

The construction industry is evolving rapidly, and those who stay ahead of the trends will be best positioned for long-term success. From digital transformation and sustainable building practices to modular construction and supply chain resilience, the future of construction cost management is full of opportunities to improve efficiency, reduce costs, and deliver better results for clients.

By embracing new technologies, staying flexible in the face of economic challenges, and fostering collaborative relationships with clients and stakeholders, project managers can navigate the complexities of cost management and ensure the success of their projects in an ever-changing industry.

Conclusion: Mastering the Art of Cost Escalation Management

Throughout this book, we've explored the many facets of managing cost escalations in construction—from identifying the root causes of cost increases to implementing proactive strategies that minimize their impact. If there's one key takeaway, it's this: cost escalation management is both an art and a science. It requires a combination of careful planning, real-time decision-making, and strong leadership to keep projects on budget and ensure long-term success.

While no two construction projects are exactly alike, the principles and strategies outlined in this book provide a solid foundation for managing cost escalations in a variety of scenarios. By focusing on documentation, risk management, and clear communication, you can reduce the uncertainty that often accompanies construction projects and build stronger, more resilient teams.

Key Takeaways for Managing Cost Escalations

As we wrap up, here are some of the most important lessons to keep in mind when managing cost escalations:

1. **Be Proactive, Not Reactive**: The best way to manage cost escalations is to anticipate them before they happen. By conducting thorough pre-construction assessments, building contingency budgets, and investing in the right technology, you can mitigate the impact of unexpected costs.
2. **Documentation is Critical**: Detailed documentation isn't just a best practice—it's essential. Keeping thorough records of contracts, change orders, daily logs, and communications helps you justify budget increases and maintain transparency with stakeholders.
3. **Foster Strong Relationships**: Whether it's with suppliers, clients, or your internal team, strong relationships are key to managing cost escalations. Build trust by communicating clearly and frequently, negotiating fair contracts, and working collaboratively to find solutions.
4. **Leverage Technology for Better Control**: The construction industry is evolving rapidly, and technology is at the forefront of this change. Use project management software, predictive analytics, and other tools to gain real-time insights into your costs, streamline processes, and make smarter decisions.
5. **Stay Adaptable**: Flexibility is crucial in construction. Projects rarely go exactly as planned, and cost escalations can be hard to predict. By staying adaptable and focusing on solutions rather than problems, you can navigate challenges effectively and keep your project moving forward.

Looking Ahead: The Future of Cost Management

The construction industry is entering a new era, one that's defined by innovation, sustainability, and collaboration. As these trends continue to reshape the way projects are managed, the ability to control costs will become even more critical to success.

Digital tools, sustainable building practices, and modular construction are just a few of the trends shaping the future of construction. By staying ahead of these developments and adopting forward-thinking strategies, you'll be better equipped to manage costs in an increasingly complex and competitive industry.

Final Thoughts: Building a Foundation for Success

Cost management is at the heart of every successful construction project. It's what allows you to stay on track, deliver value to your clients, and ensure that your business remains profitable in the long term. But managing costs isn't just about crunching numbers—it's about leadership, communication, and building a team that's committed to excellence.

By applying the strategies in this book, you'll be well-prepared to handle cost escalations with confidence and deliver projects that exceed expectations. Whether you're a project manager, contractor, or construction business owner, mastering the art of cost escalation management will set you apart in an increasingly competitive industry and help you build a strong foundation for long-term success.

Thank you for taking the time to read this book and for your dedication to improving the way construction projects are managed. I hope the insights and strategies shared here have inspired you to take a more proactive and thoughtful approach to managing cost escalations, and I wish you the best of luck in all your future projects.

Credits & Acknowledgments

Some images and portions of this book were created with the assistance of AI technology.